THE WIMP-O-METER'S GUIDE TO

illustrated by Dave Smith

JUNGLE SURVIVAL

by Tracey Turner

BARRON'S

First published as *The Wimp's Guide to Jungle Survival* in 2013 by Franklin Watts, a division of Hachette Children's Books, a Hachette UK company.

Text © Tracey Turner 2013
Illustrations by Dave Smith
© Franklin Watts 2013
Cover design by Cathryn Gilbert
Layout by Jonathan Hair

First edition for North America published in 2014 by Barron's Educational Series, Inc.

All inquiries should be addressed to:
Barron's Educational Series, Inc.
250 Wireless Boulevard
Hauppauge, New York 11788
www.barronseduc.com

ISBN: 978-1-4380-0397-9

Library of Congress Control Number: 2013943507

Date of Manufacture: January 2014
Manufactured by: B12V12G, Berryville, VA

Printed in the United States of America
9 8 7 6 5 4 3 2 1

CONTENTS

INTRODUCTION

There's nothing wrong with being a wimp. It makes perfect sense to be scared when, for example, you encounter a jaguar in the undergrowth or find yourself surrounded by thousands of toxic insects.

There's a wimp inside all of us, and he or she is there for a very good reason. From poisonous frogs to killer plants, there's a surprisingly wide variety of dangers lurking in the jungle . . .

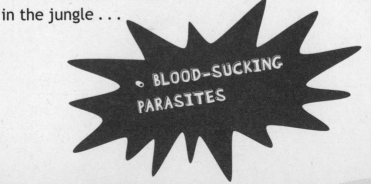

· BLOOD-SUCKING PARASITES

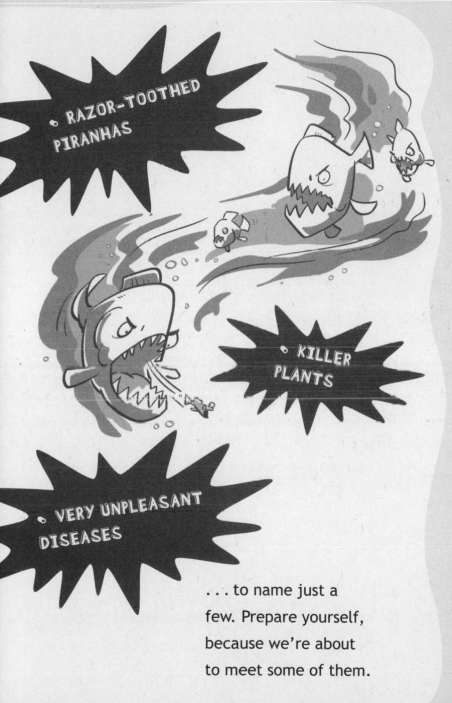

RAZOR-TOOTHED PIRANHAS

KILLER PLANTS

VERY UNPLEASANT DISEASES

. . . to name just a few. Prepare yourself, because we're about to meet some of them.

Since we're entering the jungle, remember to bring:

- clothes that cover you up (to protect you from biting insects and plants with vicious thorns)

- water purification tablets (to protect you from deadly water-borne diseases)

- a toiletry bag with soap and toothpaste (to stop you from becoming a biohazard— the jungle is bacteria heaven)

- matches (to start a fire for boiling water and cooking)

• a hammock (tents are no good since the forest floor is crawling with all sorts of things you don't want to share a bed with)

• a mosquito net (to keep out biting bugs while you sleep—see page 42)

• some food and water and containers for collecting water (you don't want to dehydrate or starve)

There, that's probably reassured you. Now that you're ready, it's time to fearlessly strike out into uncharted territory and discover all sorts of shudder-inducing details about jungle perils. With any luck, you should survive . . . if you harness the power of your inner wimp.

SURVIVING

Imagine you've been dropped off in the jungle. As you look around the dense, thorny undergrowth, a column of vicious-looking ants marches past. This is no place for a wimp! But at least you've read the introduction to this book and you've come prepared...

Water

Whether you like it or not, you'll have to find water to drink, because you won't survive without it. It's probably already occurred to you that it rains a lot in jungles and (aptly named) rain forests, and there should be plenty of rivers around, so you're in luck.

Dave, are you seeing this?

Yeah, that shirt is terrible.

FACTS WIMPS NEED TO KNOW

FINDING WATER TIPS

If you take water from a river, stream, or pool, always boil it and use water purification tablets. There are all sorts of horrible diseases you can get from germs in the water (see page 79).

BOILED WATER

It's a good idea to boil rainwater you've collected before you drink it, too, just in case something has gone to the bathroom in it when you weren't looking.

BAMBOO WATER

If you can't find a river and it's not raining, you can get water from bamboo. Check bamboo stems by tapping them. The ones that sound denser are likely to have water in them. Cut into the stem, collect the water in a container, and purify the water, just in case. Be careful around bamboo, though—stems that are close together can fly apart when they're cut. Slivers of bamboo are razor sharp and could spear you.

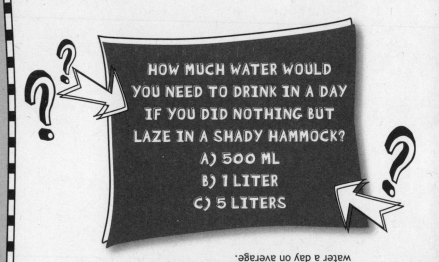

HOW MUCH WATER WOULD
YOU NEED TO DRINK IN A DAY
IF YOU DID NOTHING BUT
LAZE IN A SHADY HAMMOCK?
A) 500 ML
B) 1 LITER
C) 5 LITERS

Answer: B) 1 whole liter, even if you're just snoozing. People lose 2 to 3 liters of water a day on average.

Bamboo is a type of grass, but not like the kind you'd find on a football field. It can measure 138 feet tall and grow up to 3 feet in a day!

13

BELIEVE IT OR NOT. . .

Fish contain freshwater, especially bigger ones—the water is along the fish's spine. You'll need to gut it and remove the spine, then drink the liquid. If you're really desperate, you could always suck on an eye— animal eyes contain water. Fish eyes are quite small, but if you're about to dig in to roast wild boar, don't forget to pop out the eyes and give them a good suck. Mmmmm.

Answer: C) The frogs store water in their bodies and can be squeezed to give drinking water.

Shelter

If you were thinking of pitching a tent, think again. Have you looked at the forest floor? It's literally crawling with bugs, plus there's all that undergrowth to contend with. You'll have to sleep in a hammock.

FACTS WIMPS NEED TO KNOW

HANGING A HAMMOCK

- Find two sturdy trees about 8 feet apart, away from water and paths made by animals.
- Make sure you hang your hammock above any floodwater line, or find somewhere else.
- Secure your hammock to the trees with rope.
- Rig up a mosquito net so that you will be completely covered when you get in.
- Tie a tarp or large, broad leaves over the top of the hammock to keep off the rain.
- Climb into the hammock.
- Fall out.
- Get in again.

TERRIFYING TRUE TALES

Wimps take heart: it's possible to survive in the jungle even if you're **injured, alone, and wearing a short dress**. Seventeen-year-old Juliane Koepcke woke up in the middle of the Peruvian rain forest in 1971, still strapped to her plane seat.

Her plane had been struck by lightning and crashed, and Juliane was the only survivor. She had cuts and bruises, and a broken collar-bone, but she could walk. She set off wearing only a short dress and one shoe, which she used to test the ground in front of her for snakes. All she had to eat were a few candies she'd found at the crash site.

She walked for ten days and eventually found a boat and a deserted hut. She was rescued the next day: some men took her to the nearest town in the boat, and she was airlifted to a hospital. Juliane made a complete recovery in Germany, but she returned to Peru to work as a scientist researching rain forest bats.

Food

However famished you're
feeling, remember
that finding food in
the jungle can
be dangerous.

HUNTING ANIMALS

Are you sure about this?
It's not easy to hunt an
animal, and some of them
might end up hunting you.
But if you insist . . .

Tapirs are found in the jungles
of Central and South America
and Southeast Asia.

Tapirs look a bit like pigs with a sort of short trunk (but they're actually related to horses). They're about 3 feet high and 6$\frac{1}{2}$ feet long, and apparently they're quite tasty. But they're also strong and fast, and spearing one can be a messy and bloody business. **Bleurgh!**

Baby tapirs have stripes and spots and are incredibly cute. Sadly, they are hunted by poachers for their hide.

BELIEVE IT OR NOT...

Although tapirs are vegetarian and not usually aggressive, a Malay tapir at the Oklahoma City Zoo attacked a keeper and bit off her arm in 1998.

Peccaries (a type of wild pig found in Central and South America) and **wild boar** (found in jungles around the world) are also tasty, but they are a lot more dangerous than tapirs. They can be very aggressive and have been known to kill people.

You could also try fishing, but watch out for **caimans, piranhas,** and **electric eels** (see pages 74, 59, and 61). To avoid being attacked, maybe it's best to stick to a vegetarian diet . . .

Jungle Fruits and Veggies

Be careful when picking and eating anything in the jungle. Only eat plants you can identify and that you're absolutely sure about. You might find plenty of tasty things you recognize, such as bananas, mangos, figs, and avocados. Young bamboo shoots can be tasty too.

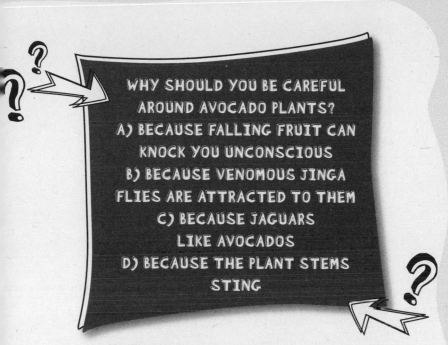

WHY SHOULD YOU BE CAREFUL
AROUND AVOCADO PLANTS?
A) BECAUSE FALLING FRUIT CAN
KNOCK YOU UNCONSCIOUS
B) BECAUSE VENOMOUS JINGA
FLIES ARE ATTRACTED TO THEM
C) BECAUSE JAGUARS
LIKE AVOCADOS
D) BECAUSE THE PLANT STEMS
STING

Answer: C) Surprisingly, jaguars love avocados—it's the only type of fruit or vegetable that they eat; otherwise, they're strict carnivores. By the way, there's no such thing as a jinga fly.

What Not to Eat

On the other hand, besides delicious fruits and veggies, there are loads of jungle plants that look tasty but could kill you. For example:

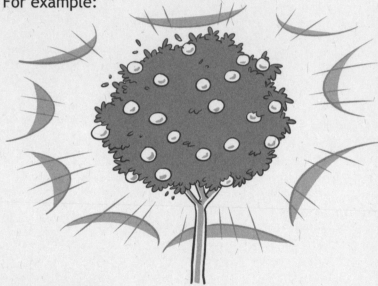

STRYCHNINE:

This innocent-looking small tree, found in tropical forests around the world, has oval leaves and fruit that resemble oranges. However, the seeds contain the poison strychnine, which is **DEADLY**.

DUCHESNEA:

This Asian plant has red fruit that look very similar to strawberries, but they have one major difference: if you eat them, they can **KILL YOU**.

I'm sooooo tasty!

PANGI:

This is a tall tree, found in Southeast Asia, with heart-shaped leaves and brown, pear-shaped fruit. The fruit might look good to eat, but in fact it's **POISONOUS**.

These are just three examples—there are plenty of other poisonous plants in the jungle. But if you're about to starve to death, you'll have to test for poison . . .

TESTING FOR POISON: ARE YOU HARD ENOUGH?

TEST 1

Crush a bit of the plant you want to test. If it smells of almonds or peaches, **don't eat it.** It's probably best to avoid plants that have white sap, too, as many of them are poisonous.

TEST 2

Squeeze a little of the plant's juice onto your skin. If it irritates it, **don't eat the plant.**

TEST 3

If the plant passed the first two tests, try these steps. If your lips or mouth feel tingly or sore at any stage, **don't eat the plant.** Wait a few minutes after each step before going on to the next one:

- try a little of the juice first on your lips,
- then the corner of your mouth,
- then the tip of your tongue,
- then under your tongue,
- then chew a small piece.

Swallow a small piece of the plant. Wait five hours, without eating or drinking anything else. If you don't experience gas, stomach pain, or sickness. . .
then the plant is safe to eat.

More Perilous Plants

Jungle plants can be dangerous in other ways—
vines and creepers have sharp thorns, bamboo
can shatter into sharp splinters, and some
plants' sap contains toxins that can irritate
the skin. There's one jungle plant that you
definitely don't want to touch.

The stinging tree (also known as gympie gympie), found in northeastern Australia and Indonesia, looks ordinary but is very nasty indeed.

It has poisonous hairs on its heart-shaped leaves that are extremely painful, and the pain lasts for months. There's even one record of the plant killing someone.

I thought you said the "singing" tree!

Now that you've found water, shelter, and food (which hopefully hasn't killed you), you're ready for anything the jungle has to throw at you. **There are just one or two hazards to look out for...**

JUNGLE ANIMALS

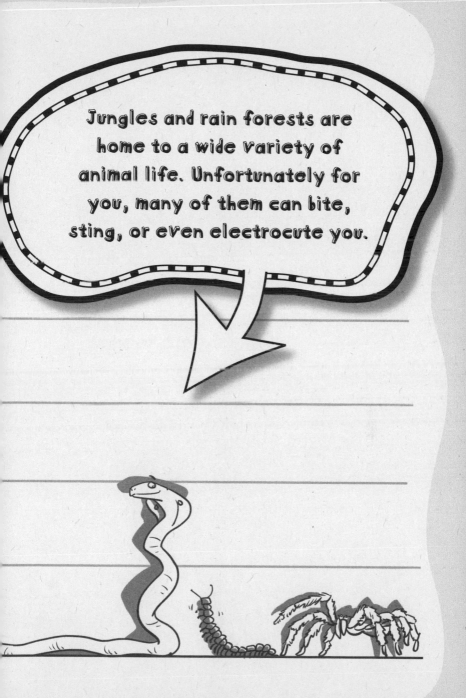

Creepy Crawlies

The type of animal you're most likely to meet in the jungle is the kind that crawls into your shoe or buzzes in your ear.

The bulldog ant from Australia holds the world record for the most dangerous ant. Its venomous bite can kill!

BULLET ANTS

Bullet ants are found in South American rain forests. They're up to an inch long and are dark reddish-brown in color. But the most remarkable thing about them is their sting: it is incredibly painful. Wimps beware, because the pain is supposed to be as fierce as being shot by a bullet, hence the name. It can make victims vomit and pass out. In fact, there are lots of ants in the jungle that can give a very painful sting, so keep away from them. And it's another good reason not to sleep on the forest floor.

Bullet Ant

TERRIFYING TRUE TALE

The Satere-Mawe tribe in Brazil has an initiation rite for young men involving bullet ants. First, thirty or so ants are put to sleep using a natural sedative, then they're woven into a mitten made out of leaves, with their stingers facing inwards.

The unfortunate young man then puts the mittens on each hand and waits for the ants to wake up. The ants bite the man's hands for ten agonizing minutes, then the gloves are removed. The pain, which is almost unbearable, gets worse as time goes on and continues for a full twenty-four hours.

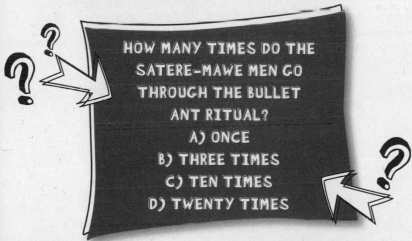

HOW MANY TIMES DO THE SATERE-MAWE MEN GO THROUGH THE BULLET ANT RITUAL?
A) ONCE
B) THREE TIMES
C) TEN TIMES
D) TWENTY TIMES

Answer: D) Could these people be the least wimpy in the entire world?

*Translation: "This really, really stings, but I've got to pretend it doesn't hurt!"

FACTS WIMPS NEED TO KNOW

ESSENTIAL INFORMATION ON OTHER CREEPY CRAWLIES

BEES

In the jungle, bees can be dangerous, and even fatal. Some of the bees in South America were introduced

from Africa in the 20th century. They are more aggressive than other bees. Usually it's easy to avoid a swarm of bees, but in the jungle you're surrounded by undergrowth. If you're stung by enough of them, even if you're not allergic to bee stings, you'll die.

CATERPILLARS

If you brush up against or touch some caterpillars, it can cause a very painful burn or rash. The hairs of hairy bag shelter caterpillars are particularly nasty.

HAIRY MOTHS

In Southeast Asian jungles, rice borer moths are small and brown with two dots on their wings.

If they land on you, don't brush them off: tiny hairs can get under your skin, causing a painful sore that can last for weeks.

GIANT CENTIPEDES

Up to a foot long, reddish-brown, and extremely creepy, giant centipedes can

give a painful bite.
The bite can even kill
people who are
allergic to the
venom.

SCORPIONS

Relax! Most
scorpions aren't
dangerous to
humans. The really
big ones with huge
pincers, like the emperor scorpion (which is
the world's biggest), only have a sting like a
wasp's, and most jungle scorpions won't hurt
you much either—the more dangerous ones are
smaller and tend to live in deserts.

LEECHES

These slimy bloodsuckers
can slurp five times their
own body weight in blood.

They're fairly harmless, and their bite is
painless. But you do run the risk of infection
if you've been bitten lots of times, so it's best
to get them off. Don't pull them, as you might
leave pieces of their mouthparts stuck in your
skin—**urrggh.** Try pouring fruit juice or salt on
them first.

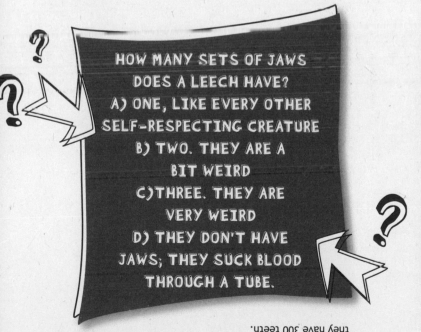

HOW MANY SETS OF JAWS
DOES A LEECH HAVE?
A) ONE, LIKE EVERY OTHER
SELF-RESPECTING CREATURE
B) TWO. THEY ARE A
BIT WEIRD
C) THREE. THEY ARE
VERY WEIRD
D) THEY DON'T HAVE
JAWS; THEY SUCK BLOOD
THROUGH A TUBE.

Answer: C) They are very weird. And
they have 300 teeth.

BUZZING THINGS

Did you just hear an annoying whining sound? It's probably a mosquito. You will meet many of them in the jungle. Most are active at night, but some come out to suck your blood during the day—there is no escape, and they are definitely out to get you.

Mosquito bites can cause a bad skin reaction and become infected. But, worst of all, mosquitoes spread diseases, some of which can be fatal (find out about them on pages 80 and 81). Make sure you apply plenty of insect repellent, cover up as much of your skin as possible, and sleep under a mosquito net.

Spiders

It might come as a relief to know that there aren't very many venomous spiders to be found in the jungle, and the ones that are venomous aren't all that dangerous . . .

SCARY
SPIDER
FREE
ZONE!

Oh! Except for the Brazilian wandering spider, which is **big and aggressive and can kill you** (for more on that, see *The Wimp's Guide to Killer Animals*).

WORLD'S BIGGEST SPIDERS

Goliath tarantulas, the world's biggest venomous spiders, live in burrows in the jungles of South America. They're enormous (a foot across) and hairy (watch out, because the spider might flick its hairs at you in defense, and they can sting). They're just about the meanest looking spiders you can imagine. But if you see one, you don't need to run away screaming. They're not very dangerous—their venom isn't powerful enough to make you ill, let alone kill you.

They're in competition with the non-venomous **giant huntsman spiders**, from Laos in Southeast Asia, for being the world's biggest spiders.

BELIEVE IT OR NOT...

The Pirahã tribespeople of Venezuela catch, toast, and eat goliath tarantulas as tasty snacks and sometimes take them on hunting trips as a packed lunch. The spiders' fangs can be used as toothpicks afterwards.

Oh, no! Toasted spider again!

Big Cats

The big cats you're most likely to meet in a jungle are tigers (in the jungles of Asia) and jaguars (in South America). Both are fierce, strong carnivores with powerful jaws. And sharp claws. And enormous teeth. **Arghhhh!**

A WIMP'S WORST NIGHTMARE

You thought wandering off into the heart of the Amazon rain forest was probably a bad idea. It's hot, humid, and full of biting insects, and you're exhausted and scratched from fighting your way through the undergrowth. Sudden screeches and squawks make you jump. What was that? Is that a pair of yellow eyes in the gloom? Suddenly a big cat springs out and pins you to the forest floor before you have time to scream . . .

Nice kitty...

Actually, being pounced upon by a jaguar in the Amazon is very unlikely. But when they do attack humans, it's usually fatal.

FACTS WIMPS NEED TO KNOW

JAGUAR VITAL STATISTICS

• Jaguars are found in Central and South America, especially in the Amazon Basin. They vary a lot in size. The biggest are up to about 265 pounds and nearly 6½ feet long. The larger ones tend to live further south.

• Jaguars share a common ancestor with tigers, lions, and leopards.

• They have the most powerful bite of any big cat (even a tiger's). It's strong enough to chomp through a turtle's shell.

- Jaguars are good swimmers and prey on fish, caimans, and turtles, as well as land animals such as deer and peccaries (wild pigs).

- The word "jaguar" comes from a Native American word that means "he who kills with one leap."

WHAT IS A BLACK PANTHER?
A) A BLACK JAGUAR
B) A BLACK MOUNTAIN LION
C) A BLACK LEOPARD
D) A MYTHICAL BEAST

Answer: A) About six in every hundred jaguars are black. If you look closely, you can still see the spots that other jaguars have (although getting too close is not recommended). By the way, mountain lions, or cougars, are smaller than jaguars and live in the Americas too (though not as far south as jaguars), and leopards are spotted like jaguars but live in Africa, Asia, and China.

TIGER VITAL STATISTICS

• Tigers, like jaguars and other big cats, don't usually see people as prey. But particular tigers have been known to become man-eaters, **so watch out!**

• Tigers are the biggest of the big cats. They weigh up to a whopping 660 pounds and can be more than 10 feet long.

• There are six different kinds of tigers around today—the biggest are Siberian (Amur) tigers—but the kind you're most likely to see in an Asian jungle are Bengal tigers, which account for around half of all tigers.

BALI TIGER

CASPIAN TIGER

JAVAN TIGER

There used to be three other kinds, but they died out in the 20th century.

White Bengal tigers are sometimes born in the wild, and some of those are born without stripes.

Gorillas (and monkeys)

Huge, hairy, and potentially lethal, lowland gorillas lurk in rain forests in Central and West Africa. The biggest gorillas—mature males, or "silverbacks"—can be 400 pounds and 6 feet tall, so you definitely do not want to upset one. Luckily, gorillas are vegetarian and not usually aggressive, though attacks on people have happened.

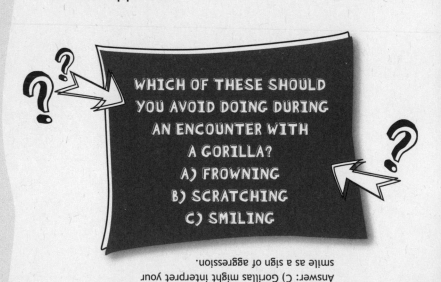

WHICH OF THESE SHOULD
YOU AVOID DOING DURING
AN ENCOUNTER WITH
A GORILLA?
A) FROWNING
B) SCRATCHING
C) SMILING

Answer: C) Gorillas might interpret your smile as a sign of aggression.

To avoid enraging a gorilla, keep away from their babies and don't make eye contact, scream, run away, or throw anything.

BELIEVE IT OR NOT...

In Delhi, India, groups of rhesus monkeys have become famous for their violent attacks and were responsible for the death of the deputy mayor of Delhi, S.S. Bajwa, who fell off a balcony trying to defend himself from them in 2007.

Killer Birds

In the jungle, even birds can be lethal . . .

CASSOWARY BIRDS

Cassowary birds are large, flightless birds, a bit like emus, with bright blue-and-red crests on their heads. They live in the rain forests of northern Australia and New Guinea.

FACTS WIMPS NEED TO KNOW

THREE REASONS TO AVOID A CASSOWARY

- They are big—6¹/₂ feet tall and up to 176 pounds in weight.

- When they're surprised or cornered, they can attack—and they can run at up to 31 mph.

- They have massive claws! The inner claw on each foot is up to 5 inches long and could easily rip you open.

- Cassowary birds attack by striking out in front of them with their feet.

HARPY EAGLES

If you're in the jungle in Central or South America, watch out for harpy eagles—one of the world's most powerful birds of prey. They hunt various mammals, including monkeys, some of them almost as big as the birds themselves.

RRAWWK

Poor monkeys! Don't try to hunt these birds of prey for food, though, as many are protected by law. For example, killing a Philippine eagle in Southeast Asia will cost you a heavy fine and up to 12 years in prison.

A cameraman was attacked by a harpy eagle when he got too close to her nest. He was OK, despite the bird's 5-inch claws.

Piranhas

Piranha fish are the stuff
of wimp nightmares: they have a fearsome
reputation for their ability to strip the flesh
from a cow in a matter of seconds, leaving
only a skeleton. But, in fact, they're nowhere
near as scary as that.

IT'S NOT TRUE!

FACTS WIMPS NEED TO KNOW

PIRANHAS

• Piranhas live in lakes and rivers in South America, especially in the Amazon River.

• There are lots of different kinds of piranhas: the most ferocious is the meat-eating red-bellied piranha, which can be 13 inches long and has the sharpest teeth and strongest jaws.

• Even red-bellied piranhas won't reduce you to a skeleton if you dip a toe in the Amazon: they don't prey on big animals—mostly leaving people and other large animals alone, mostly...

Piranhas are at their most dangerous in the
dry season, when they can become trapped
in isolated pools without enough to eat.
They can turn a bit ugly then. The teeth of
a red-bellied piranha are scalpel-sharp: they
could give you a very nasty bite. There are
no records of piranhas attacking and killing
humans. **Phew!** There are plenty of people
missing fingers, toes, and other bits and
pieces because of them, though... **Gulp!**

Electric Eels

Think twice before you
go fishing in the Amazon and Orinoco rivers
in South America: lurking in murky, sluggish
waters, electric eels await their prey.
Actually, so do caimans and piranhas. But it's
the electric eels you should be worrying about
the most.

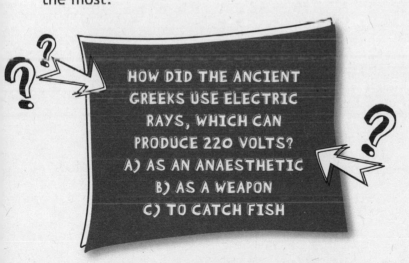

HOW DID THE ANCIENT
GREEKS USE ELECTRIC
RAYS, WHICH CAN
PRODUCE 220 VOLTS?
A) AS AN ANAESTHETIC
B) AS A WEAPON
C) TO CATCH FISH

Answer: A) They used the electrical
charge to stun patients before
operations or during childbirth!

ELECTRIC EELS AND HOW TO AVOID THEM

• Electric eels are big: up to 8$\frac{1}{2}$ feet long and 44 pounds in weight.

• They feed on fish and other small creatures, which they stun by producing a powerful electric current (without the aid of batteries). They also use electricity to shock predators.

• The electric current produced by electric eels can be as much as 600 volts—enough to kill you.

The shock from an electric eel has been known to knock a horse off its feet!

Electric eels aren't really eels at all—they're fish, related to catfish. They are common in the Amazon and Orinoco rivers.

If you have to go into the water where electric eels could be hiding, wear rubber boots and carry a stick to check the water in front of you.

Toxic Frogs

The golden poison dart frog, which lives in the Colombian rain forest, is the world's most poisonous creature. It's 2 inches long, yet it contains enough poison to kill at least ten adult humans. It's only dangerous if you touch it, though—the deadly poison seeps through the pores in your skin and into your bloodstream.

If you touched a golden poison dart frog and then touched your mouth, or if the frog's poisonous skin touched a wound on your body, the poison would almost certainly kill you within minutes.

The Choco and Cofan people of Colombia rub arrows or darts onto the frogs' backs to collect the poison. If they shoot an animal with the poisoned dart, it'll drop dead instantly. Although the golden poison dart frog is the most poisonous, many other toxic frogs live in the jungles and rain forests of South America. So don't touch any small, brightly colored frogs, OK?

Snakes

There are lots of snakes to be found in jungles around the world. Many of them are venomous and well camouflaged—a potentially fatal combination. Here are a few to keep an eye out for . . .

BUSHMASTER

Bushmasters are found in Central and South America and are one of world's most venomous snakes. They're big, too—up to 10 feet long.

The bushmaster is nocturnal, so you're unlikely to come across one while it's hunting, unless you're creeping around in the dark. During the day you might disturb a sleeping one, though, so watch out and always wear sturdy footwear!

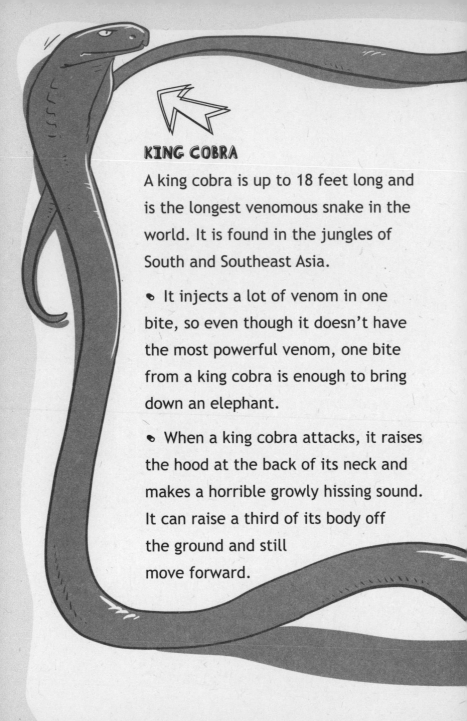

KING COBRA

A king cobra is up to 18 feet long and is the longest venomous snake in the world. It is found in the jungles of South and Southeast Asia.

• It injects a lot of venom in one bite, so even though it doesn't have the most powerful venom, one bite from a king cobra is enough to bring down an elephant.

• When a king cobra attacks, it raises the hood at the back of its neck and makes a horrible growly hissing sound. It can raise a third of its body off the ground and still move forward.

CORAL SNAKE

There are different types of coral snakes, found in Africa, Asia, and the Americas, ranging from 16 inches to about 64 inches long. They're brightly colored, usually three different colors, in broad stripes around their bodies. If you are bitten by a snake that fits this description, get to a hospital quickly— the bite won't be very painful, but the venom is powerful and can stop your heart or your breathing within a few hours.

There are plenty more venomous snakes to be found in the jungle, and there are some dangerous non-venomous snakes too . . .

SQUEEZING SNAKES

The biggest snake in the world is the green anaconda, found in the jungles of South America. It's a constricting snake: it doesn't have venom, but it kills its prey by coiling around it, squeezing tighter and tighter, until the animal can no longer breathe. **Gack!**

Green anacondas can be up to 30 feet long (that's as long as a bus!) and weigh up to 507 pounds.

Pardon me. Which way to the Serpentine?

Their cousins, **reticulated pythons**, are found in Southeast Asia and can be almost as big as anacondas. Both types of snakes are good swimmers and live in or near water.

Big constricting snakes prey on animals as large as deer—and they can open their mouths wide enough to swallow the prey whole!

TERRIFYING TRUE TALES

Toninho Negreiro, a wildlife documentary presenter, was filming in the Colombian rain forest in 2009. He was shown an anaconda by a guide, who then let the snake go. Rather unwisely, when everyone stopped for lunch, Toninho decided to go and catch the snake again for another look.

The snake grabbed ahold of his arm with its
100 sharp teeth and began to wrap itself
around his body. It took five strong men
to get the snake off him.

Crocs, Alligators, and Caimans

Crocodiles, alligators, and caimans lurk menacingly in tropical jungle rivers all over the world. Caimans will usually leave you alone, unless you step on one by mistake, but alligators and crocodiles won't. They will happily have you for breakfast.

WAAAAAAHH!!

FACTS WIMPS NEED TO KNOW

CROC VITAL STATISTICS

• Caimans, crocodiles, and alligators are all crocodilians.

• Alligators can grow up to $16\frac{1}{2}$ feet long, caimans are smaller, and the biggest crocodiles—saltwater crocodiles—can be a whopping 20 feet long.

• The smallest crocodilian is the West African dwarf crocodile, which is up to 6 feet long.

• Alligators and caimans tend to have a U-shaped snout, while crocodiles have a V-shaped snout.

• Crocodiles tend to be more aggressive toward people than alligators.

Relax, though, because you're not very likely to be eaten by an alligator. No, you're much more likely to fall foul of a deadly disease . . .

DISGUSTING AND DEADLY DISEASES

Fatal Jungle Diseases:

YOUR GUIDE TO THE SYMPTOMS

 = vaccine available

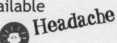 Headache

Stomach pain

High temperature

Skin rash

Backache

Vomiting

Constipation

Dry cough

Diarrhea

Aching muscles

Shivers

78

TYPHOID

Plus either 🐸 or 🐸

Things are not looking good. If typhoid isn't treated, it gets worse: you might have trouble working out what's real and what's imaginary.

You get typhoid from bacteria in food or water, and it can be fatal if you don't go to a doctor.

YELLOW FEVER

After the first stage, 15 percent of people develop even more horrible symptoms, including yellow skin (which is a sign of liver damage), blood in poo, bleeding from mouth or eyes, and kidney failure. The disease is caused by a virus spread by the bite of a particular mosquito. There's no cure, and 50 percent of people with yellow fever die.

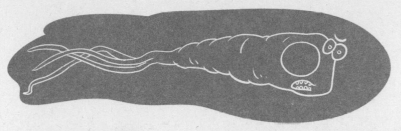

TETANUS

Symptoms include stiffness in jaw muscles—so that it's difficult to open the mouth—sweating, a rapid heartbeat, and maybe difficulty swallowing and breathing. Tetanus is caused by bacteria entering an open wound.

MALARIA

There are different types of malaria, but in addition to the symptoms above, sufferers can also experience hallucinations and loss of appetite. It's spread by anopheles mosquitoes. There's no vaccine but you can take anti-malarial tablets, which is a good idea since the disease can kill.

Yes, it just gets more and more horrible.

TYPHUS

With that impressive list of symptoms, you won't be surprised to hear that typhus can be fatal. The disease is caused by bacteria spread by lice or fleas—specifically, the poo of the lice and fleas, which gets into the bloodstream when the victim scratches.

FLEA

Other fatal diseases include:
- cholera
- Chagas disease (transmitted by the kissing bug)

- dengue fever (transmitted by yet another particularly nasty type of mosquito)
- Weil's disease, which you get from drinking water that contains animal pee (especially rat pee)

Oh, and if you've been bitten by an animal—especially one that's acting a bit oddly you might well have contracted rabies. Just to be on the safe side, get to a hospital, because if you don't and symptoms have appeared (sensitivity to light, difficulty swallowing, hallucinations, being afraid of water . . . the list goes on), it means **certain death.**

Even More Jungle Sickness

Here's one final condition to get worried about. **Warm Water Immersion Foot** is very nasty and develops when your feet are constantly wet. The soles of the feet become white, wrinkled, and painful, and must be allowed to dry out and heal. They can become **EXTREMELY** sore if you're not careful . . .

TERRIFYING TRUE TALES

Yossi Ghinsberg and three friends were searching for a "lost" tribe in the heart of the Amazon rain forest in Bolivia in 1982. After a while they split up, Yossi traveling by raft with his friend Kevin, and the other two on foot. Yossi was swept over a waterfall and became separated from Kevin.

He survived on his own for three weeks, eating fruit and the eggs of jungle fowl, and once had to scare off a jaguar by setting fire to insect spray. His feet were so painful with Warm

Water Immersion Foot that he said he tipped biting ants over his head to distract himself from the pain.

Eventually, Kevin, who had found his way to safety, came to look for Yossi with some others and rescued him. Sadly, the other two friends were never found.

Some Unpleasant Parasites

The jungle is crawling with parasites on the lookout for a nice, juicy mammal. All of them are absolutely disgusting—**so keep reading!**
Here is a small but utterly horrible selection:

CATTLE GRUBS OR BERNES

These are fly larvae. The fly drops the larva onto the skin of an animal, and the larva burrows inside, leaving a breathing hole. You'll know you have one if you have a red lump on your skin that . . . wriggles.
Urrrgghh!

Treatment involves putting adhesive tape over the breathing hole—the larva dies and can be removed. You just have to try not to think about it too much while the maggot is in its death throes underneath the surface of your skin.

LARVA MIGRANS

These are worms that can burrow underneath the surface of human skin. You'll know they're there by the little red track marks they make as they travel around—they look like tiny red rivers under the skin. You get them from areas where animals have pooped.

LICE AND TICKS

Lice live on humans, pooping away as they go. If you scratch where the lice have bitten, the poop gets into your bloodstream and can give you the deadly disease typhus. Ticks embed themselves in the skin—don't grab their body to pull them out, as you might leave the head behind. Use a pair of tweezers to grab their head or mouthparts as close to the skin as possible. Wash the wound with soap if you can. Ticks can give you some nasty diseases.

Last Word

You've been very brave. You've faced horrible diseases, giant anacondas, and wormy things wriggling around underneath your skin. Now you're armed with vital information that will help you survive in hostile jungle conditions. Hopefully, you'll now know how to hang a hammock, remove a variety of parasites, and avoid death by electric eel. Now that you have nothing to fear from the jungle, you might want to think about some other scary things for a wimp to worry about . . .

Your Wimp Rating

Answer these questions with **"yes"** or **"no."**
How many do you answer
"yes" to? Add up the number
to generate your very own
wimp rating on page 93—go on,
how tough are you **really?**

1. You're with a friend who is filming anacondas in the Colombian rain forest. She wants to do a close-up with you and the snake. You say . . .

2. Cassowary birds are nothing to be scared of; they're just big chickens. Do you agree?

3. You're staying with some Pirahã tribespeople in Venezuela. They offer you a packed lunch— do you eat it?

4. You're lost in the jungle and start feeling hungry. Do you begin hunting for wild boar?

5. You put together a hammock from a blanket you have. Do you manage to climb into it the first time without falling out?

6. Mosquitoes are just flying bugs; they can't hurt you. Do you agree?

7. You're on a safari to a gorilla colony when a gorilla steps out of the jungle in front of you. Do you wave at it and smile?

8. The Satere-Mawe tribe invites you to take part in an initiation ceremony. Do you accept the invitation?

9. A massive scorpion wanders into your empty shoe. Do you shake your shoe until it comes out?

10. Jaguars don't scare you— they're just like big kitties with a bad temper. Do you agree?

How many questions did you answer "yes" to?

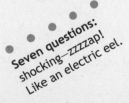

Three questions: you're a novice wimp—you're on the path to great wimpiness.

Four questions: you're a wannabe wimp—keep trying.

Five questions: halfway to becoming a wimp idol.

Six questions: up in your hammock with a sleeping jaguar.

Seven questions: shocking—zzzzap! Like an electric eel.

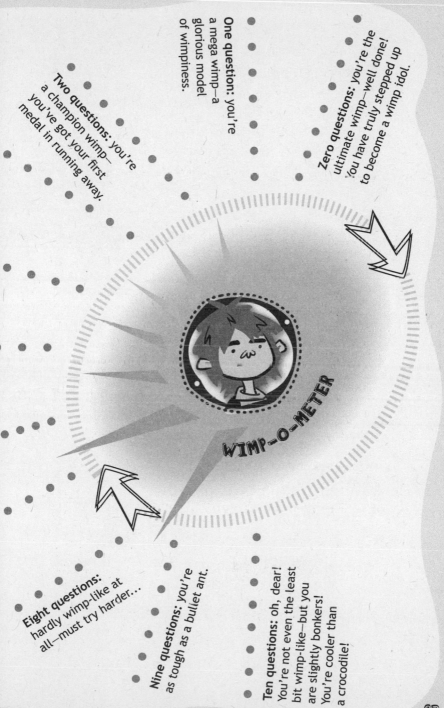

One question: you're a mega wimp—a glorious model of wimpiness.

Two questions: a champion wimp— you've got your first medal in running away.

Zero questions: you're the ultimate wimp—well done! You have truly stepped up to become a wimp idol.

WIMP-O-METER

Eight questions: hardly wimp-like at all—must try harder...

Nine questions: you're as tough as a bullet ant.

Ten questions: oh, dear! You're not even the least bit wimp-like—but you are slightly bonkers! You're cooler than a crocodile!

Glossary

Aborigine here, the people who first lived in Australia

allergic someone whose body reacts strongly to a type of food, insect bite, pollen, etc.

biohazard a risk to other people's health

carnivore an animal that eats other animals

dehydrate to lose water from the body

diarrhea a bad stomach upset

hallucination seeing something that isn't there

humid when the weather is hot and damp

infection when bacteria or viruses get into the body and start to multiply, causing damage to the body

initiation rite a special ceremony, often to welcome someone into a group (or marking entry to the adult world)

larva the young of an insect, including grubs, caterpillars, and maggots

nocturnal active at night, while sleeping or resting during the day

parasite an animal or plant that lives on other animals or plants

poacher hunters who steal or kill animals on land where they have no right to be

pore a tiny hole in the skin

sap sticky liquid that flows through plants

toxic poisonous

venom poisonous liquid

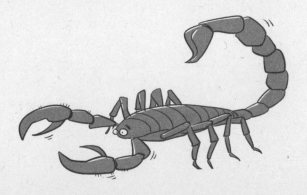

Index